D1222023

Snap books®

Beyoncé Knowles

by Jen Jones

CAPSTONE PRESS
a capstone imprint

Snap Books are published by Capstone Press,
151 Good Counsel Drive, P.O. Box 669, Mankato, Minnesota 56002.
www.capstonepress.com

092009
005618CGS10

Library of Congress Cataloging-in-Publication Data
Jones, Jen.
    Beyoncé Knowles / by Jen Jones.
    p. cm. — (Snap books. Star biographies)
    Includes bibliographical references and index.
    Summary: "Describes the life and career of Beyoncé Knowles" — Provided by publisher.
    ISBN 978-1-4296-3397-0 (library binding)
    1. Beyoncé, 1981– — Juvenile literature. 2. Singers — United States — Biography — Juvenile literature. I. Title.
II. Series
ML3930.K66J66 2010
782.42164092 — dc22   2009027789

Editor: Kathryn Clay
Designer: Juliette Peters
Media Researcher: Marcie Spence
Production Specialist: Laura Manthe

Photo Credits:
Alamy/Photos 12, 23
AP Images/Elise Amendola, 4–5; Jeff Christensen, 28; Jennifer Graylock, 7
Getty Images Inc. for the NAACP/Charley Gallay, cover
Getty Images Inc./Frank Micelotta, 26, 27; Jim Smeal/WireImage, 14;
    L. Cohen/WireImage, 9; Mark Wilson, 6; SGranitz/WireImage, 22; Vince Bucci/AFP, 17
New Line/The Kobal Collection, 21
Newscom, 19; Splash News and Pictures, 25; WENN, 13
Supplied by Capital Pictures, 29
Wikipedia, public-domain image/WhisperToMe, 10

Essential content terms are **bold** and are defined at the bottom of the page where they first appear.

Table of Contents

CHAPTER 1

A Powerful Performance

Flash back to January 20, 2009. President Barack Obama prepared to take office. On this day, one of the most memorable campaigns came to a close with a star-studded celebration in Washington, D.C. At the center of the event was Beyoncé Knowles. She had been asked by President Obama to sing Etta James's song "At Last" at the Neighborhood Ball.

After being introduced by Oscar winner Denzel Washington, Beyoncé took the stage in an elegant Armani Prive gown. As Beyoncé sang the classic tune, the president and first lady danced nearby. Overcome by emotion, Beyoncé fought back tears as she sang for the new president. At the end of the song, Beyoncé blew a kiss to the first couple.

Beyoncé said that singing for President Obama was the best moment of her career.

This wasn't Beyoncé's first presidential performance. In 2001, she sang for President George W. Bush's **inauguration** as part of Destiny's Child. But singing at Obama's inauguration was especially rewarding for Beyoncé. She had spent months before the election traveling with her husband, Jay-Z, to promote Obama's campaign. She even postponed a performance in Japan to be in the United States on election night. And now she was singing for the nation's first black president. Not too shabby for a young Texan girl who started out singing and dancing in her backyard.

Beyoncé sang "America the Beautiful" for Obama's inaugural celebration at the Lincoln Memorial.

inauguration — the ceremony in which the president is installed in office

Tina Knowles (left) has designed many of Beyoncé's outfits.

Designer Duds

Besides making catchy music, Beyoncé is also known for her eye-catching fashion choices. She gets this passion for fashion from her mom, Tina.

A costume designer and stylist, Tina has been outfitting Beyoncé since her days in Destiny's Child. Tina works hard to make sure Beyoncé stands out.

In 2004, Beyoncé and her mom joined forces to design a clothing line. The clothes combine a modern flair with a vintage style. They called the clothing line House of Deréon after Tina's mom, Agnes Deréon. In 2006, House of Deréon became a sister act when Beyoncé's younger sister, Solange, came on board to design a junior line.

"We wanted to take elements from my grandmother's legacy — the beaded lace, lush colors, fine fabrics — and mix them with clothes from my mother's generation and my generation."
— Beyoncé told *Ebony* magazine in 2005.

Starting Out Shy

Before Beyoncé made it big, she was just a shy girl growing up in Houston, Texas. On September 4, 1981, Beyoncé Giselle Knowles was born to Tina and Mathew Knowles.

Many people wonder how Beyoncé's parents chose her unique name. Beyoncé was chosen in honor of Tina Knowles' **maiden name**, Beyince. Although Beyoncé didn't always appreciate her special name, she has grown to love it.

Both Tina and Mathew had very successful jobs. Tina owned one of the largest hair salons in Houston. Mathew was a top salesman at Xerox. Though Beyoncé's parents were career-oriented, their main focus was on family. In 1986, Tina and Mathew welcomed another daughter, Solange. Solange would grow up to be a performer just like her big sis.

maiden name — the last name that a married woman used before she was married

Beyoncé and her younger sister, Solange (left), have always been close.

Beyoncé attended the High School for the Visual and Performing Arts in Houston.

Growing Up Beyoncé

When you watch Beyoncé on stage, it's hard to picture her as anything but outgoing. Yet Beyoncé was a shy child who chose to keep to herself. She was an excellent math student and enjoyed helping her classmates solve tricky problems. But Beyoncé rarely raised her hand in class. She shrank in her seat when teachers called on her. She usually walked with her head down to avoid drawing attention to herself.

Music and dance brought Beyoncé out of her shell. At the age of 7, she started studying with Ms. Darlett. Ms. Darlett taught Beyoncé not only about dance, but also about confidence and hard work.

At Ms. Darlett's urging, Beyoncé entered a local talent show. Beyoncé took the stage and sang "Imagine" by John Lennon. The audience was shocked to see the shy youngster transform into a pint-sized powerhouse. Beyoncé received a standing ovation. She soon realized she was meant to perform. She began taking voice lessons and singing in the church choir.

"[Ms. Darlett] was the first person who convinced me I had talent. She is the reason I started performing."
— Beyoncé in the book *Soul Survivors*

Girl's Tyme

Soon Beyoncé was a regular on the talent show scene. She also joined the singing group Girl's Tyme. There she met future Destiny's Child members LaTavia Roberson and Kelly Rowland. Kelly and Beyoncé became fast friends. Kelly later moved in with the Knowles family. The two girls could always be found rehearsing and laughing. From the backyard to Tina's hair salon, every place they went turned into a stage.

After years of trying to get a record deal, it seemed that Girl's Tyme was finally about to hit the big time. In 1992, the group earned a spot on *Star Search*, a popular TV talent competition. Beyoncé and her bandmates dressed in colorful satin jackets and jean shorts. They performed a rap song for the judges. But their efforts weren't enough to beat the rock band they were pitted against.

Kelly Rowland (middle) and Beyoncé (top right) were members of Girl's Tyme before forming Destiny's Child.

Original members of Destiny's Child included LeToya Luckett, Beyoncé, LaTavia Roberson, and Kelly Rowland (left to right).

A Date with Destiny

After the *Star Search* loss, Beyoncé, Kelly, and LaTavia formed their own group. LeToya Luckett completed the new group. Beyoncé's dad was convinced the girls would be successful. He even quit his job to manage the group. Beyoncé's mom helped the girls choose a name. They tried The Dolls, Cliché, and Somethin' Fresh, but nothing seemed to fit. After reading a Bible passage, Tina suggested "Destiny." Mathew added the word "Child."

Though the group later became superstars, the road was rocky at first. Destiny's Child was signed to Elektra Records when Beyoncé was just 14 years old. But the excitement was short-lived. Just eight months later, the group was dropped from the label without ever releasing an album.

Though discouraged, the girls decided to give it one more try. They performed for Columbia Records executives in 1996. A few weeks later, the girls were hanging out at Tina's salon when they got the good news. They had been offered a new record deal — and another shot at stardom.

CHAPTER 3

Fame Comes Calling

Beyoncé spent two years hard at work to make the Destiny's Child self-titled **debut** album. The group's first hit was "No, No, No." It was an unforgettable moment for Beyoncé and Kelly when they first heard the song on the radio. The two were picking up Solange from school when some familiar notes came over the airwaves. The girls cranked up the volume and sang along.

Bittersweet Success

The group's success wasn't all good news. It meant Beyoncé would have to make many sacrifices. She quit attending regular school in ninth grade and started working with a **tutor**. Because Mathew quit his job, the family was down to one income. The Knowles had to sell their home.

debut — the first time something is shown or performed
tutor — a teacher who gives lessons to just one student

The green dresses worn by Destiny's Child at the 2001 Grammys were designed by Tina Knowles.

But the sacrifices paid off. In 1999, the group's second album, *The Writing's on the Wall*, came out. The album sold millions of copies and became one of the year's best-selling releases. In 2001, Destiny's Child won two Grammy awards for the hit song "Say My Name." The group loved its newfound star status. They were even invited to Whitney Houston's 35th birthday party.

Drama, Drama, Drama

It wasn't all fun and games behind the scenes. Shortly after the release of the group's second album, members LeToya and LaTavia quit. Both girls sued Mathew and claimed he took more than his share of the group's earnings. They also accused him of giving special attention to Beyoncé and Kelly. LeToya and LaTavia eventually settled their lawsuit. They were replaced by Michelle Williams and Farrah Franklin. But after just five months, Farrah also left Destiny's Child.

The timing of Farrah's departure couldn't have been worse. Destiny's Child was set to perform in Australia. Beyoncé, Kelly, and Michelle were nervous about how fans would react to the change. Yet the Australia show proved there was no need to worry. The group delivered a knockout performance.

Destiny's Child did its best to move on. In 2001, the group's third album, *Survivor*, debuted at number one on the *Billboard* 200 album chart. More than 12 million albums were sold worldwide. The smash hit "Survivor" was inspired by the group's struggles with its former members. As part of the *Charlie's Angels* soundtrack, the video for "Independent Women, Part 1" was an instant MTV hit.

Mathew Knowles (middle) continues to manage Beyoncé.

Life on the Road

Beyoncé loved being in the spotlight, but touring often took its toll. She got very little sleep and zero downtime. She ate meals in dressing rooms and limousines. Much of her travel time was spent writing new songs. Beyoncé's talent and hard work didn't go unnoticed. The American Society of Composers, Authors, and Publishers named Beyoncé Songwriter of the Year in 2002.

CHAPTER 4

Flying Solo

As the lead singer for Destiny's Child, Beyoncé received much of the attention. Hollywood executives began to take notice. In 2001, Beyoncé was asked to show off her acting skills in the MTV musical *Carmen: A Hip-Hopera.* This was her first movie role and her first time away from family and friends. For three months Beyoncé sang, danced, and acted. She missed Kelly and Michelle, but she enjoyed the chance to grow as a performer.

Soon to follow was an offer to co-star opposite Mike Myers in *Austin Powers: Goldmember.* Beyoncé was excited about her new role as secret agent Foxxy Cleopatra. She impressed the cast and crew with her singing and acting talents.

"My heart was beating fast, my mouth was dry, my palms were clammy. I had to wipe my hands on my pants before I shook hands with Mike Myers."
— Beyoncé in the book *Soul Survivors.*

Beyoncé enjoyed working with Mike Myers (left) in *Austin Powers: Goldmember*.

Dangerously in Love

In 2003, Beyoncé released her first solo album, *Dangerously in Love*. Jay-Z was a guest rapper on several tunes, including the first single "Crazy in Love." Fans fell crazy in love with the song. The song was number one on the *Billboard* Hot 100 singles chart for eight weeks. **Critics** also praised the album. Beyoncé was voted one of *Entertainment Weekly's* Top Entertainers of 2003. The following year, she won five Grammys.

Destiny Fulfilled

Despite her solo success, Beyoncé wasn't finished with the group that started it all. In 2004, Destiny's Child reunited to release *Destiny Fulfilled.* The success of the album allowed the trio to go out on a high note. In 2005, Destiny's Child announced the group would be parting ways after a farewell world tour. Artists Usher and Rihanna performed a medley of Destiny's Child songs at the 2005 World Music Awards. That night Destiny's Child was also named best-selling female group of all time.

In 2004, Beyoncé won five Grammys and tied the record for most awards won by a female artist.

critic — someone whose job it is to review a CD, book, or movie

Eddie Murphy, Anika Noni Rose, Beyoncé, and Jennifer Hudson (left to right) starred in *Dreamgirls*.

Dream Girl

In 2006, Beyoncé made a splash as Deena Jones in *Dreamgirls*. *Dreamgirls* is a flashy musical that tells the story of a 1960s singing group. The movie earned many awards, including two Golden Globe nominations for Beyoncé. She was nominated in 2007 for Best Performance in a Musical or Comedy and Best Original Song. *Dreamgirls* also received the most Oscar nods of any film that year.

CHAPTER 5

Shining Star

From award shows to concerts to film sets, Beyoncé is always on the go. And her busy schedule doesn't stop once the spotlight fades. When not performing, Beyoncé attends photo shoots, costume fittings, and promotional appearances. She also works hard behind the scenes by writing and producing many of her songs. And like any star, Beyoncé spends a lot of time doing interviews.

> "I'm never gonna go on stage or do a video and not work until my feet are blistered, and until I'm basically, I can't walk any more. I always give, and I do that because I know how lucky I am, to do my job."
>
> — Beyoncé in an interview with the *Associated Press*.

Tommy Hilfiger (right) teamed up with Beyoncé to launch a new fragrance.

Along with performing, Beyoncé also stays busy as a model and spokesperson. In 2002, Beyoncé landed a major deal with Pepsi. In 2004, she received $4.5 million from fashion designer Tommy Hilfiger to represent the fragrance True Star. Beyoncé has also been in commercials for L'Oreal cosmetics, Emporio Armani Diamonds perfume, Nintendo DSi, and American Express. Combined with her album sales, Beyoncé's annual salary tops $85 million.

Jay-Z (right) celebrated Beyoncé's 25th birthday at the 40/40 Club in New York City.

Crazy in Love

Despite her status in the spotlight, Beyoncé describes herself as an extremely private person. She's happiest among friends and family. And in recent years, that group has expanded to include Jay-Z. Beyoncé and Jay-Z married on April 4, 2008, in a small, private wedding in New York City. The couple has also paired up professionally. Together they've made music videos and written popular songs. Yet they are still careful to keep their relationship out of the media spotlight.

Though secretive about their relationship, Beyoncé and Jay-Z make no secret of their love for each other. Jay-Z spent half a million dollars on Beyoncé's 23rd birthday bash at New York's Soho House. Beyoncé rented a private plane for Jay-Z's 37th birthday to whisk him away on a four-day vacation.

Yet it would be hard to top Beyoncé's 25th birthday celebration in 2006. Held at Jay-Z's club in Manhattan, the party attracted stars like Ne-Yo, Rihanna, and Nicole Richie. Beyoncé was already riding high, as she had performed her hit "Ring the Alarm" earlier that evening at the MTV Video Music Awards. Her special night was completed with an unforgettable gift from Jay-Z — a Rolls Royce convertible worth $1 million.

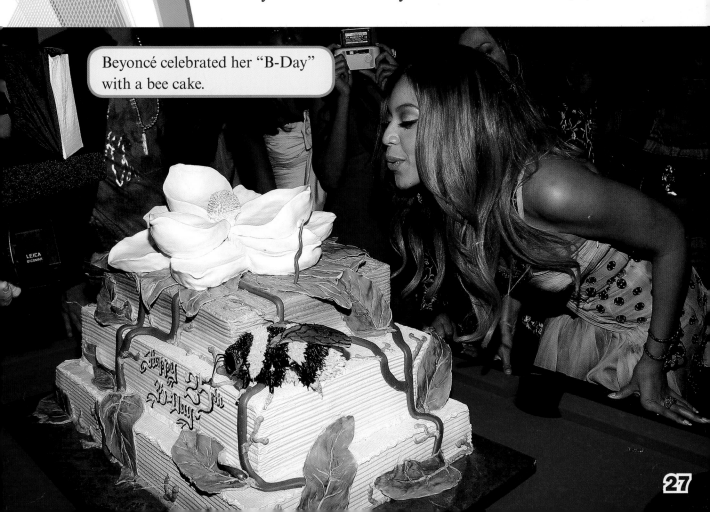

Beyoncé celebrated her "B-Day" with a bee cake.

Beyoncé performed with Justin Timberlake (right) during the 2008 Fashion Rocks show.

It Takes Two

Though Beyoncé is no longer part of a singing group, she still loves to share the singing stage. Some of her biggest hits have been duets with other stars. She performed "Baby Boy" with reggae-style rapper Sean Paul and "Beautiful Liar" with sassy songstress Shakira. Other singers Beyoncé has joined forces with include Justin Timberlake, Luther Vandross, and Jay-Z. Beyoncé even performed a bluegrass version of her song "Irreplaceable" with the country duo Sugarland.

Bright Future

As Beyoncé continues her solo career, she seeks to balance her love of singing and acting. Beyoncé recorded 16 new songs for her third solo album. Released in November 2008, *I Am…Sasha Fierce* is her most personal album to date. The two-disc set featured popular hits like "Halo" and "If I Were a Boy." Yet the song that had everyone talking is "Single Ladies (Put a Ring On It)." The tune's catchy dance video inspired imitations by everyone from Justin Timberlake to Joe Jonas. The song also topped *Rolling Stone*'s list of the 100 Best Singles of 2008.

Beyoncé has also decided to continue her acting career. In the 2008 film *Cadillac Records*, she played famous blues singer Etta James. Beyoncé also co-starred in the thriller *Obsessed*. Audiences loved the film's suspenseful love triangle plot. Box office numbers showed the film made close to $70 million.

Beyoncé's across-the-board success has made an undeniable mark on pop culture. And she shows no signs of stopping. Whether it's singing, acting, dancing, or designing, fans can't wait to see what Beyoncé will do next.

Beyoncé (seen here portraying Etta James) said she would like to do more acting in the future.

Glossary

album (AL-buhm) — a collection of music recorded on a CD, tape, or record

critic (KRIT-ik) — someone whose job is to review a CD, book, or movie

debut (day-BYOO) — the first time something is shown or performed

inauguration (in-aw-gyur-RAY-shun) — the ceremony in which the president of a country is installed in office

maiden name (MAYD-uhn NAYME) — the last name that a married woman used before she was married

medley (MED-lee) — a musical piece that consists of bits and pieces of different songs

tutor (TOO-tur) — a teacher who gives lessons to just one student or a small group of students

unique (yoo-NEEK) — one of a kind

Read More

O'Mara, Molly. *Beyoncé.* Stars in the Spotlight. New York: PowerKids Press, 2007.

Tracy, Kathleen. *Beyoncé.* A Blue Banner Biography. Hockessin, Del.: Mitchell Lane, 2005.

Waters, Rosa. *Beyoncé.* Hip-Hop. Broomall, Pa: Mason Crest, 2007.

Internet Sites

FactHound offers a safe, fun way to find Internet sites related to this book. All of the sites on FactHound have been researched by our staff.

Here's all you do:

Visit *www.facthound.com*

FactHound will fetch the best sites for you!

Index